Front cover: Konza Prairie Research Natural Area
in Riley County. STEVE MULLIGAN

Back cover: The scarcity of timber led farmers to
carve fence posts of rock, such as these in
Russell County. STEVE MULLIGAN

Title page: Along Highway 61 in Reno County.
JOHN C. AVERY

ISBN 1-56037-186-2

Photographs © by John C. Avery, Charles Gurche,
and Steve Mulligan as credited

© 2001 Farcountry Press

For more information on our books write:
Farcountry Press, P.O. Box 5630, Helena, MT
59604 or call: (800) 654-1105 or visit
montanamagazine.com

Created, produced, and designed in the United
States. Printed in China.

Kansas is to many people a no man's land; nothing there. Popular belief is that, should you have the misfortune to need to travel through Kansas, do it at night because there is nothing to see anyway. Although Kansas, as with the other plains states, is sometimes boring and monotonous, it has a simple, fundamental beauty that is not found anywhere else. Wide open spaces, the ability to see for miles, beautiful, incredible sunsets, the friendliest people, a serene peacefulness that allows deep soul searching. There are not many crowds, big cities, or road-raged drivers. There is something very special about Kansas.

While it primarily is an agricultural state, the wide open spaces allow for wildlife to flourish and for photographers to roam freely capturing the simple beauty of the state. The rock formations left here by the inland sea millions of years ago, the rolling Flint Hills, the Smoky Hills, and the Gypsum Hills. The beauty of the various farm crops cast against an incredible sky, or a rainbow. The colorful wildlife.

To some, I suppose, Kansas is an impossible challenge, photographically speaking. We don't have mountains, seashores, things people think appropriate for a "tourist" state. But Kansas has a very special beauty all its own, even if it is true, perhaps, that you must look a bit closer and harder than elsewhere. I was born and raised in Kansas, and after being gone for fifteen years, I returned and looked at it in a far different manner than ever before. But being a photographer when I returned caused me to view the state as if I had never been here before. Although there are many other places in this country that I love, Kansas is my home, and I will always see its fundamental beauty.

—JOHN C. AVERY

I grew up on the eastern edge of Kansas, not far from Kansas City. Our family was lucky to live along a small creek, which came to life each spring with a chorus of toads and frogs. Beyond the stream, a hardwood forest covered the hillside, and from my bedroom window I watched the changing seasons. Powerful thunderstorms were common in the spring and early summer, and I can remember counting seconds between flashes and crashes to calculate a storm's distance. From the window, I would watch as the flashing bolts illuminated the stream as it rose to a torrent and spilled out of its banks into our yard.

With friends and family, I explored other places farther from home in the Kansas countryside. A trip to the Flint Hills revealed a landscape powerful in its vast openness and simplicity. In fifty miles, the land had

Flint Hills prairie in central Kansas. CHARLES GURCHE

changed from forests to grasslands. There was a true Western feel from the distant horizon and boundless sky. I was enamored with these plains.

I left Kansas to live farther west but returned often, several times for a photography assignment for Smithsonian Books to shoot natural areas in the state. I discovered a wonderful variety that is missed by those blazing across the state on Interstate 70. In Kansas, east meets west and its landscape holds badlands, waterfalls, buffalo herds, yucca and cacti, strange rock formations, deciduous forests, and sandbar-lined rivers. This collection of images will merely scratch the surface of the treasures that can be found in the Kansas landscape.

—CHARLES GURCHE

Kansas is one of my very favorite states to photograph, and continues to provide new and exciting subject matter as time passes. The sere high plains are dotted with wonderful badlands, while the tallgrass prairie is imbued with a subtle, expansive beauty. The eastern woodlands, with numerous streams and rivers braiding through them, continue to provide me with new and exciting scenery. As my explorations into the Kansas landscape continue, there seems to be no end to the wonderful scenery, and a limitless supply of compositions.

—STEVE MULLIGAN

Indian grass in Konza Prairie. STEVE MULLIGAN

Cottonwood snags at Clinton Lake State Park. STEVE MULLIGAN

Wildflowers along Skyline Scenic Drive, near Council Grove. CHARLES GURCHE

Morning tiptoes into Lake Scott State Park. CHARLES GURCHE

Sign that a beaver has been interrupted in his home-building along Marais des Cygnes River in Linn County. STEVE MULLIGAN

Left: Layers of ancient ocean bottoms in Mushroom Rock State Park, southwest of Salina. STEVE MULLIGAN

Below: Topeka, founded in 1854, became the state capital in 1861. The current governor's mansion, seen here, is the state's second. JOHN C. AVERY

Above: During a flood, Mill Creek left this debris high in a Wabaunsee County tree. STEVE MULLIGAN

Facing page: Butterfly milkweed splashes the land with color. STEVE MULLIGAN

Above: Grain elevators, like these at Minneola, are the castle towers of the plains. JOHN C. AVERY

Facing page: Cheyenne Bottoms Wildlife Refuge, near Great Bend, holds habitats for waterfowl, marsh birds, and raptors including bald eagles. STEVE MULLIGAN

Above: ...and the cows in the corn. JOHN C. AVERY

Below: 'Nuff said. JOHN C. AVERY

Facing page: Winter turns Sand Arroyo Creek into a composition in gray and white. STEVE MULLIGAN

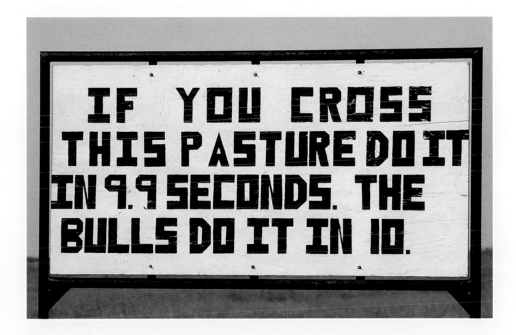

Near Oakley, the Monument Rocks and Chalk Pyramids are monoliths formed on the bottom of an ancient sea, then carved by eons of wind and rain. STEVE MULLIGAN

Yucca blooms on the Scott County shortgrass prairie. STEVE MULLIGAN

Missouri River bottomlands near Fort Leavenworth are rich in vegetation. STEVE MULLIGAN

Rich grasses along Illinois Creek. STEVE MULLIGAN

Above: The water is up and so's the wind, but that won't keep a serious fisherman away from Clinton Lake. JOHN C. AVERY

Facing page: Once held in a glacier's grinding grasp, these "erratic" rocks landed in Wabaunsee County when the ice melted. STEVE MULLIGAN

Above: Black-eyed Susans say it's summer. CHARLES GURCHE

Facing page: Around one hundred million years ago, the substance of the Chalk Pyramids was shells protecting sea creatures. CHARLES GURCHE

Just a whisper of autumn on Crawford County maples and sunflowers. STEVE MULLIGAN

Rising above Kanopolis Lake in its namesake state park, bluffs blush at sundown. CHARLES GURCHE

The breaks of the Arikaree River are just inside Kansas's northwest corner.
STEVE MULLIGAN

Above: The Flint Hills shape puny human projects like Interstate 70.
JOHN C. AVERY

Right: Ring-necked pheasants, an Asian species imported to the United States, like to live in farmland—and so flourish in Kansas.
JOHN C. AVERY

Facing page: Soft spring weather in Riley County. STEVE MULLIGAN

Z Bar/Spring Hill Ranch barn in Tallgrass Prairie National Preserve. STEVE MULLIGAN

McPherson County's Maxwell Game Preserve.

Winter wheat sprouts up in Cheyenne County. STEVE MULLIGAN

Harvest time means long hours in the cab for Kansas farmers. JOHN C. AVERY

View from the top in Chase County Courthouse, Cottonwood Falls, which was designed by the same architect as the state capitol. JOHN C. AVERY

Cheyenne Bottoms, Barton County. STEVE MULLIGAN

Above: One rock offers up another to Mushroom Rock State Park visitors. CHARLES GURCHE

Facing page: Combine a sandstone arch and the photographer's eye to make a perfect frame—at Monument Rocks. CHARLES GURCHE

Geary County pond on a peaceful gold and green day. CHARLES GURCHE

At home in the Sunflower State. JOHN C. AVERY

Above: A daytime moon approaching Rock City sandstone in Ottawa County. STEVE MULLIGAN

Right: Tallgrass textures by winter, Konza Prairie. STEVE MULLIGAN

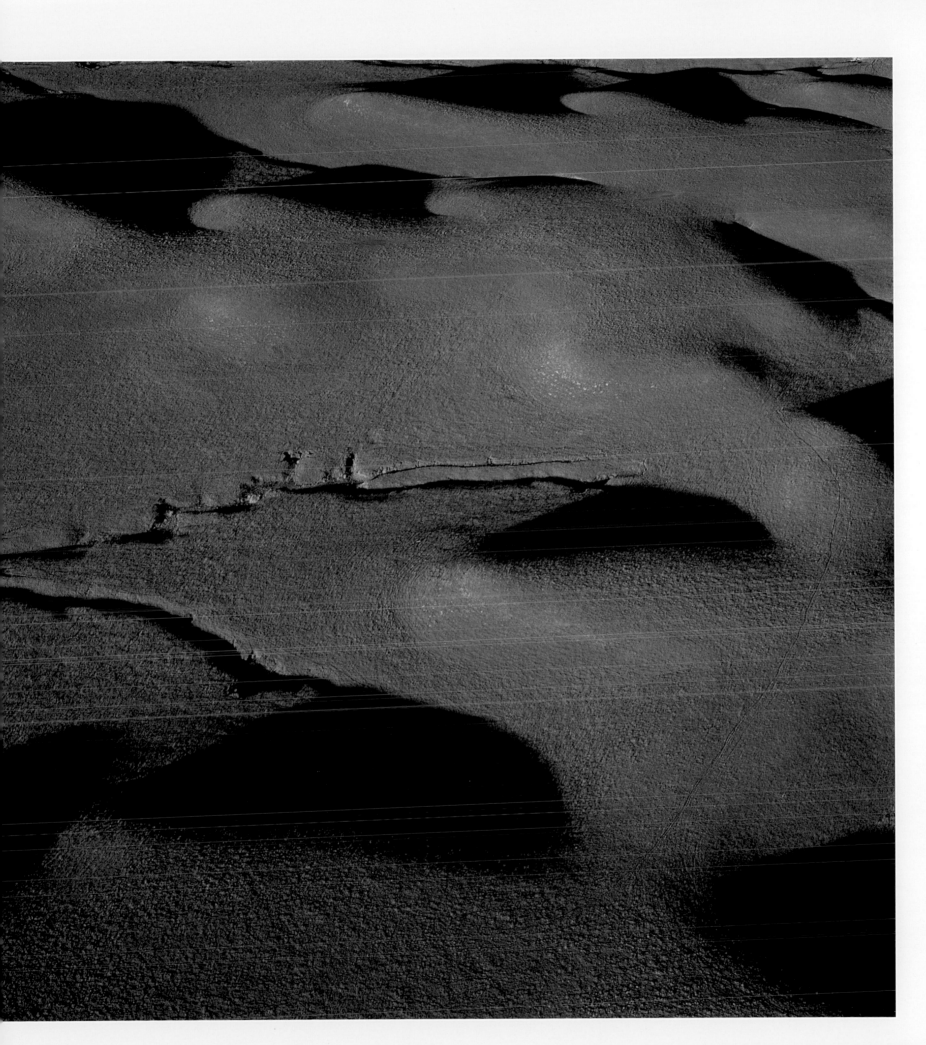

Above: Farming veterans of many a season, near Lake City. JOHN C. AVERY

Facing page: Butterfly weed flourishes in Sand Hills State Park. CHARLES GURCHE

A cooling interlude on Bourbon County's Wolf Pen Creek. STEVE MULLIGAN

Burr oaks like this are among the tree species of Breidenthal Reserve near Lawrence. STEVE MULLIGAN

Sundown silhouette of Castle Rock in Gove County. STEVE MULLIGAN

Tauy Creek's Ireland sandstone in Douglas County. STEVE MULLIGAN

Prairie riches of different kinds, near Hays. JOHN C. AVERY

Left: "Ike," President Dwight David Eisenhower, is portrayed as he appeared when appointed supreme commander of World War II's Allied Expeditionary Force in this statue at the Eisenhower Center, Abilene. JOHN C. AVERY

Below: Fort Larned, near Larned, was built in 1859 to protect Santa Fe Trail travelers; today the national historic site features living history on summer weekends. STEVE MULLIGAN

Close in among Monument Rocks. JOHN C. AVERY

Tuttle Creek Lake nestles in the Flint Hills near Manhattan. STEVE MULLIGAN

Pillsbury Crossing on Deep Creek, Wabaunsee County. STEVE MULLIGAN

Right: Grain elevators and trains—the route to market for the nearly 500 million bushels of Kansas wheat per year. JOHN C. AVERY

Below: Stormy weather for Salina. JOHN C. AVERY

Above: Spotlight on the land near WaKeeney. JOHN C. AVERY

Facing page: Purple coneflower in the Flint Hills. STEVE MULLIGAN

Millions of American bison, like these in Scott County, once ranged across Kansas land. STEVE MULLIGAN

Winter symphony east of Wichita. JOHN C. AVERY

Above: The Z Bar/Spring Hill Ranch's intriguingly shaped main bedroom in the ranch headquarters area of Tallgrass Prairie National Preserve. STEVE MULLIGAN

Facing page: Jack Frost's paintbrush has been busy in Leavenworth County. STEVE MULLIGAN

The Custer House in Fort Riley dates from 1855, and was named to honor Lt. Col. George Custer, who never lived here. JOHN C. AVERY

In Wichita, Old Cow Town Museum holds nearly four dozen buildings restored or reproduced from ones that saw the city's cowtown heyday, 1865-1880. JOHN C. AVERY

Little Jerusalem Badlands, Gove County. STEVE MULLIGAN

Above: Pomona Lake State Park, south of Topeka, offers outdoor recreation both summer and winter. STEVE MULLIGAN

Facing page: Wildflowers turn tallgrass lands into a prairie garden. STEVE MULLIGAN

Kansas leads the United States in wheat production. JOHN C. AVERY

Round Prairie Community Church, Leavenworth County, at sunset. STEVE MULLIGAN

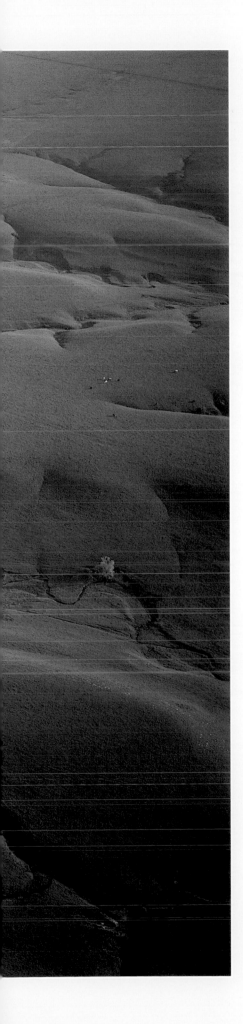

Above: Soapwort blossoms carpet the land surrounding cottonwood trees. STEVE MULLIGAN

Left: Springtime reaches the Flint Hills. STEVE MULLIGAN

Above: Field of gold: coreopsis blossoms along Flint Hills Scenic Drive. CHARLES GURCHE

Facing page: Mill Creek races wide and fast. STEVE MULLIGAN

Cloud drama colors the Kansas River. STEVE MULLIGAN.

Testament to natural weathering in Russell County's Rocktown Natural Area. STEVE MULLIGAN

Above: Poison ivy conquers Ireland sandstone in Breidenthal Reserve. STEVE MULLIGAN

Left: Feel the summer humidity in the Flint Hills. CHARLES GURCHE

Above: Victoria residents worked from 1908 through 1911 building their Cathedral of the Plains, finishing it with stained glass windows imported from Germany. JOHN C. AVERY

Facing page: Kanopolis Lake twilight. CHARLES GURCHE

Above: The sun rises reluctantly on a Konza Prairie winter day. STEVE MULLIGAN

Facing page: Pastel portrait of the Chalk Pyramids. CHARLES GURCHE

Near Lake City. JOHN C. AVERY

Wilson County's Fall River. STEVE MULLIGAN

Above: Original blockhouse at Fort Hays, near the town of Hays, which dates from the time of the Civil War. JOHN C. AVERY

Below: Checking out the greener grass. JOHN C. AVERY

Facing page: Summer reflection at Pope Cave, Comanche County. STEVE MULLIGAN

Autumn mosaic afloat on Alcove Spring, Marshall County. STEVE MULLIGAN

In southeastern Kansas, this falls, the river, the county—all are named Elk. STEVE MULLIGAN

Warnock Lake in Atchison County. STEVE MULLIGAN

Tallgrass mingles with rock outcroppings
in Chase County. STEVE MULLIGAN

The Arkansas River flows through Wichita, Kansas's biggest city, which has changed with the times from a wide-open railhead cowtown to a manufacturing and financial center. JOHN C. AVERY

Nature's forces have carved limestone into fantastic shapes in the Smokey Hill River Valley. CHARLES GURCHE

Shadows invade the Arikaree Breaks. STEVE MULLIGAN

The Kansas state flower, in abundance. STEVE MULLIGAN

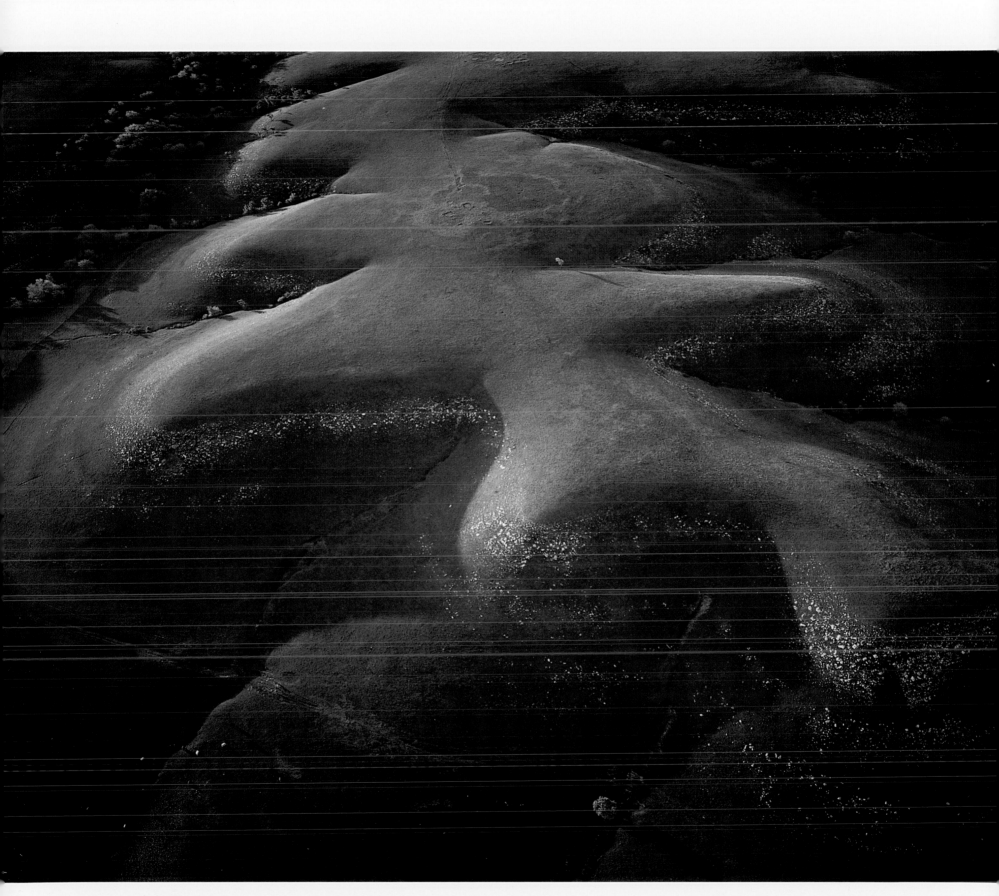

The Flint Hills emerge into spring in Geary County. STEVE MULLIGAN

Nature's bridge over Cowskin Creek in Pawnee Prairie Park near Wichita. CHARLES GURCHE

Above: A wee echo of the days when millions of cattle shipped from Kansas railheads. JOHN C. AVERY

Below: Prairie breaks in Clark County. JOHN C. AVERY

Above: Sassafras and sumac in Cherokee County's Schermerhorn Park. STEVE MULLIGAN

Facing page: Castle Rock was a landmark for Indian peoples long before emigrant wagon trains used it the same way. STEVE MULLIGAN

What visitor to Fort Larned National Historic Site doesn't image the thump of boots and the clank of spurs on this gallery? CHARLES GURCHE

Southwest of Minneapolis, Rock City's sandstone spheres range in diameter from eight to twenty-seven feet. STEVE MULLIGAN

Above: Kansas bovines, on the job. JOHN C. AVERY

Facing page: The Kansas River wends its way through Riley County. STEVE MULLIGAN

Near Hewins and the Oklahoma border, a redbud dons its spring bonnet. STEVE MULLIGAN

Left: Crisp new prairie sentinels. JOHN C. AVERY

Below: Yoder-area Amish families have a day in town.
JOHN C. AVERY

Above: Logan County aerial view. STEVE MULLIGAN

Facing page: In Cheyenne Bottoms Wildlife Area near Great Bend. STEVE MULLIGAN

Above: In Barber County's Red Hills. STEVE MULLIGAN

Facing page: Konza Prairie Research Natural Area in winter mode, Riley County. STEVE MULLIGAN

The sparkling Spring River in Schermerhorn Park. CHARLES GURCHE

Left: This killdeer chick can't be far from the rest of his noisy flock. JOHN C. AVERY

Below: Beaumont is home to the United States' last operating railroad water tower.
JOHN C. AVERY

Above: Wheat heads hang heavy, ready for harvest. STEVE MULLIGAN

Facing page: A stormy night gathers over the Kansas River. STEVE MULLIGAN

The proud sandstone Z Bar ranch house in Chase County. STEVE MULLIGAN

Smooth sumac in Lake Scott State Park, Scott County. STEVE MULLIGAN

Above: The glorious Kansas ocean. JOHN C. AVERY

Right: Gove County's Little Jerusalem Badlands. STEVE MULLIGAN

Above: A sudden flood flashes through the Missouri River Bottoms in Leavenworth County. STEVE MULLIGAN

Facing page: The Big Caney River steps over Osro Falls in Chautauqua County. STEVE MULLIGAN

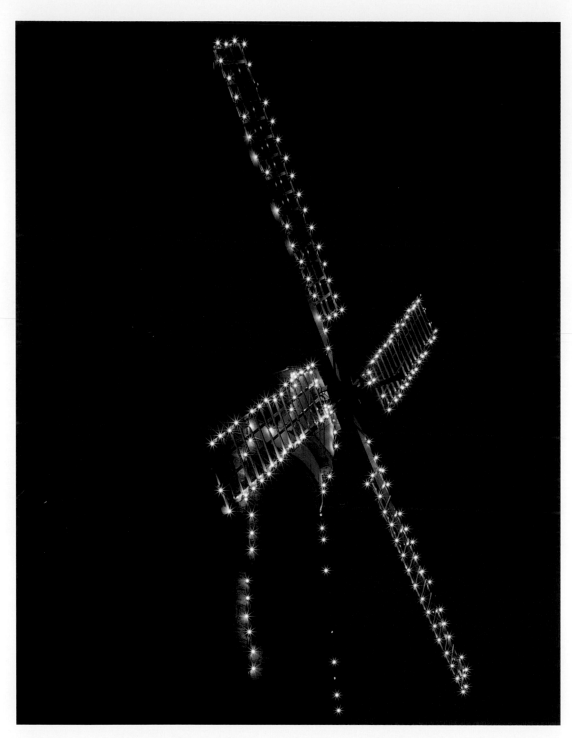

In Wamego, the reconstructed Old Dutch Mill was a custom feed and meal grinder beginning in the 1870s.
STEVE MULLIGAN

Sundown magic. JOHN C. AVERY

Above: Poison ivy snuggles up to a sycamore along Mission Creek. STEVE MULLIGAN

Right: Man-made Elk City Lake on the Elk River centers its namesake state park. STEVE MULLIGAN